# STOP THE SLAUGHTER!

A Collection of Halloween Poems

WRITTEN & ILLUSTRATED BY CATHEE ROEHRIG

Copyright © 2000 text and illustrations, "Home Grown Pumpkin Poems.....And Other Halloween Stuff"
By Cathee Roehrig

Copyright © 2008 text and illustrations, "Stop The Slaughter" by Cathee Roehrig
("Stop the Slaughter" poem is based on the copyrighted © 1988 tee shirt design/illustration by Cathee Roehrig)

All rights reserved. No part of this book may be used or reproduced in any manner whatsoever, electronic or mechanical, including photocopying, recording or any other information storage and retrieval system, without written permission from the author.

First Printing: 2008

ISBN 978-1-4196-5550-0
Library of Congress Control Number: 2008902741
Publisher: BookSurge Publishing
North Charleston, South Carolina 29418
U.S.A.

A big ol' thanks to Glenn Evans...who never gave up!

## Stop the Slaughter

Throughout the generations,
From sons and moms and daughters,
The poor pumpkin families
Need protection from the slaughter.

For each and every Halloween,
The carving does commence.
Pumpkins are then displayed
On porch, on shelf and fence.

We don't eat meat. We don't chop trees.
We have saved up every whale.
But when it comes to pumpkins,
Well, our efforts seem to pale.

For we seem to never think about
How all this carving started
And how it all eventually ends
With dear pumpkins departed.

I think that we should all go join
To save our orangey friends
And form a coalition
To stop this carving trend!!!

## Soaped Opera

Someone did a nasty deed
And took a bar of soap
And wrote a bunch of nasty words
That you couldn't show the Pope!

I really thought my car was safe
And I didn't have a worry,
But now it seems I'll have to go
And wash it in a hurry!!

## The Most of Ghosts

Mom put me in this costume,
It wasn't my first pick.
I wanted something creepy,
Mom wanted something "quick."

## A Visit to the Candy Drawer

Jim took all his candy
And put it in his drawer.
It mingled with his socks
And dropped out on the floor.

It crammed into the back
And stuck to all his shirts.
It melted from the heat
And stuck to dust and dirt.

Jim quit going in there
As it was a sticky mess,
And it was getting harder
To find some clothes to dress.

It might have mutated
Or eaten all his clothes.
Who knows what candy does
When in a drawer enclosed?

It's been in there a year
And now Jim will explore
To find out if his candy
Looks like candy anymore!

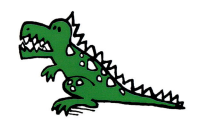

### Ding-Dong-Dog

They ring the doorbell.
    The dog goes nuts!
        It's hard to quiet
            The stupid mutt.
He barks and barks
    As I hand out sweets
        To little strangers
           From the street.
I tell my dog,
    "They're here for treats,"
        But dogs don't know
           What's under sheets
And under masks,
    All dark and scary!
        (The things that are
           So customary.)
My dog will never
    Comprehend
        That a trick-or-treater
           Is our friend!

**Garden Sweets**

Glenn took some of his candy corn
And planted it on a sunny morn.

He weeded it with a garden hoe
So it would have a chance to grow.

He gave it water and lots of sun
And couldn't wait 'til it was done.

He gave it all that it could need--
But someone ate up all the "seeds!"

## Pumpkin Rot

Pumpkins sit on porches
All orange and smooth and funny
But something changes pumpkins
When put out where it's sunny.

Their outtards all cave innards
And they wrinkle in and rot.
It's hard to know just what they were...
...'Cuz now, pumpkins they're NOT!

## Pageant Puss

I wanted something different
To do for Halloween,
So I took the family cat
And made a "beauty queen."

   He didn't like the dress.
   I couldn't style his hair.
   He acted like he hated it
   And gave a nasty glare.

      He wouldn't wear the crown.
      Then he ate up all the flowers.
      His makeup turned out crooked
      ---And it had taken hours!

         I wanted something different
         To do for Halloween,
         So I left the family cat alone...
         ...He was getting kinda mean!

### Guilt Pie for Dinner

Protesting Pam
And Striking Sam
Are in it for pumpkin rights!

So if you haven't heard
Their protesting words
Sit down to your dinner tonight

And the guilt will appear
As they scream in your ear
To remind of the pumpkin's plight...

..."HOW MANY PUMPKINS HAD TO DIE
FOR YOU TO EAT THAT PUMPKIN PIE??"

# Carvin' Marvin

I have a little pumpkin.
I call my pumpkin, Marv.
I've kind of grown attached to him,
Which makes it tough to carve.

I shed a little tear for Marv
As I cut in deep and scoop
And make a funny "cut out face"
Amidst this pumpkin goop.

Marv is smiling back at me;
A big and toothy grin.
I'm proud of my accomplishment.
First place we both could win!

But mom yells,
"CLEAN UP THIS MESS!"
So I put it all back in.

## Scaredy Cat

The cat got into my bag of treats
And ate up something he shouldn't eat.
Now he's horked up something hairy--
That's why Halloween's so SCARY!

## House Dressing

We dressed our house
For Halloween.
It was the coolest place
You've ever seen!

We added stuff
So much, so more,
We cleaned out
All the local stores!

In the trees
We hung some bats
And on the porch
Were big black cats.

Scary pumpkins
And icky spiders
Guarded candy
And our cider.

We draped some webs
Across the door
And added mist
That swirled the floor.

A witch's cauldron
Boiled with brew.
(What it was --
We have no clue!)

Blinking eyes and
Howling cackles
Brought out monsters
Stopped by shackles.

The yard filled up with
Graves and headstones
All topped off with
Creepy white bones.

We added lights
For that special glow,
And read out loud
Some works by Poe.

This year we added
So much more
That no one found
Our house's door!!

**Sick or Treat?**

All the candy we did eat
Made us full and sick of treats.

Our bellies bulged,
Our mouths did belch.
The gurgling sounds
We could not squelch.

"You ate too much,"
Our mom did say.

...But tomorrow is another day!!

## Protect our Pumpkins

Protect the little wordless ones.
Protect our pretty gourds.
Protect the pumpkins from the knife.
Protect them from the hordes.

Protect the pumpkins from the sun.
Protect them from the rain.
Protect the pumpkins when it comes
To scooping out their brains.

Protect the pumpkins on Halloween.
Protect them from the frost.
Protect them from the neighbor's dog,
Protect them at any cost!

**Moppy Halloween**

I was a witch for Halloween,
But I kinda was a flop.
We didn't have a broomstick
So I used my mother's mop.

**Rainy Ways**

Why does it always rain
As ghosts and such go out?
(When they trick-or-treat
It never is a drought!)

It gets so cold and windy
And then it starts to pour.
Their costumes getting drenched
As they go from door to door.

NEXT year, before this happens,
We really should decide--
Where should we have Halloween?
How about ---INSIDE?